Copyright © 2025 Jennifer Jones
All copyright laws and rights reserved.
Published in the U.S.A.
For more information, email info@ninjalifehacks.tv
Paperback ISBN: 978-1-63731-960-4
Hardcover ISBN: 978-1-63731-962-8
eBook ISBN: 978-1-63731-961-1

Find the Santa on Strike lesson plans at ninjalifehacks.tv

The very next day in the class,
a letter did appear.
It smelled like cocoa, looked hand-stitched,
and filled the room with cheer.

Dear children,
I love to bring you joy,
but changing lists a dozen times
is wearing down this boy!

Love,
Santa
(Seriously. Pick one!)

The kids sat quiet, one by one,
their cheeks a little red.
"I didn't mean to make him nuts,"
a girl named Gracie said.

I changed my list four times...

Miss Berry said, "Let's fix this fast, before the sleigh takes flight. We'll make a plan that's smart and kind and help him sleep at night!"

They made one list and checked it twice,
then signed it neat and bold.
No add-ons, swaps, or silly tricks.
Just wishes for toys and gold.

At home, old Santa got the notes and beamed from ear to ear. "They picked one gift and stuck with it... this might just save the year!"

Now every year they choose with care
and think before they write.
Santa smiles and sips his cocoa,
no chaos every night!

So if your wishlist starts to grow
or change a dozen ways,
just pick one gift that means the most
and make old Santa's day.

Next Up: Cupid on Strike?

Create Your Official Santa Wish List!

Pick one special thing and write a note to Santa.

My wish: _____
Why I chose it: _____
_____
What I want to say to Santa: _____
_____
_____

Write a Thank-You Note to Santa!

Make Santa smile with your words!

www.ingramcontent.com/pod-product-compliance
Lightning Source LLC
Chambersburg PA
CBHW041712160426
43209CB00018B/1814